The World at His Fingertips

The World at His Fingertips

A Story about Louis Braille

by **Barbara O'Connor**
illustrated by **Rochelle Draper**

A Carolrhoda **Creative Minds** Biography

Carolrhoda Books, Inc./Minneapolis

To Aunt Margaret with love

**Note: In French, Louis Braille's last name is pronounced BRY.
Most English speakers say BRAYL.**

Text copyright © 1997 by Barbara O'Connor
Illustrations copyright © 1997 by Carolrhoda Books, Inc.

Carolrhoda Books, Inc.
A division of Lerner Publishing Group
241 First Avenue North, Minneapolis, MN 55401 U.S.A.

Website address: www.lernerbooks.com

Library of Congress Cataloging-in-Publication Data

O'Connor, Barbara.
    The world at his fingertips : a story about Louis Braille / by Barbara
O'Connor ; illustrations by Rochelle Draper.
        p.   cm. — (A Carolrhoda creative minds book)
    Includes bibliographical references and index.
    Summary: A biography of the nineteenth-century Frenchman, accidentally
blinded as a child, who created the dot system of reading and writing that is
now used by the blind throughout the world.
    ISBN 1-57505-052-8 (lib. bdg. : alk. paper)
    1. Braille, Louis, 1809–1852—Juvenile literature. 2. Blind teachers—
France—Biography—Juvenile literature. 3. Braille—Juvenile literature.
[1. Braille, Louis, 1809–1852. 2. Blind. 3. Teachers. 4. Physically handi-
capped. 5. Braille.] I. Title. II. Series.
HV1624.B64026   1997
686.2'82'092—dc21
[B]   96-49950

Manufactured in the United States of America
2 3 4 5 6 7 – MA – 07 06 05 04 03 02

Table of Contents

1

No More Sunlight

Louis Braille sat in the doorway of his father's harness shop and watched his sisters, Catherine-Joséphine and Marie-Céline, come out of the stone farmhouse. Their colorful skirts and baskets of artichokes told him it was Thursday. Chickens squawked and scurried out of the way as Louis raced across the yard to join his family in the two-wheeled oxcart. His father, Simon-René, and brother, Louis-Simon, loaded the last of the leather harnesses, bridles, and reins onto the cart with the baskets of vegetables.

Then the Braille family headed up the steep hill to the village square.

Thursday was market day in Coupvray, a small farming village twenty-five miles east of Paris, France. Farmers and villagers from the surrounding countryside came to sell or trade fruits and vegetables, pigs and cows. Three-year-old Louis (pronounced loo-EE) loved the hustle and bustle of the market. While his father and brother set up the booth to display the leather goods they had made, Louis's mother, Monique, would lead him through the crowd to buy freshly baked bread for the ride home. Louis waved to the familiar faces in the crowd—the weaver, the tailor, the blacksmith. Usually he recognized a farmer or a winegrower who had come to buy a harness or have a bridle repaired at his father's shop.

Sometimes Louis overheard the villagers talking in serious tones, with worried faces. But he was too young to understand that times were troubled in Europe. France had been involved in several wars within the last twenty years. Now, in the spring of 1812, Napoléon Bonaparte, the emperor of France, was gathering troops to invade Russia. The villagers feared there would soon be another war.

Louis was also too young to help out with many of the chores at home. (Besides the harness shop, the

Brailles owned a small vineyard and enough land for a large vegetable garden.) But the boy was not too young for a ride on the back of the milk cow when his brother led the animal to the fields. Sometimes Louis helped Marie-Céline collect eggs in the chicken house or ran alongside Catherine-Joséphine to the washhouse by the stream.

Some days Louis sat by the kitchen fire, shelling beans with his mother, his curly blond head bowed in concentration. But the kitchen was cold and dark. His mother had whitewashed the stone walls to brighten the room, but the few small windows let in little light. Louis preferred the sunlit doorway of his father's harness shop. He loved the smell of the oiled leather and the big hides hanging from hooks in the ceiling.

Simon-René was considered one of the best harness makers in the area. With expert hands, he kneaded the oiled hides and trimmed them into strips for bridles and reins, just as his father had done before him. Simon-René planned to leave his thriving business in the hands of his oldest son, Louis-Simon, someday. As for young Louis, Simon-René had other plans. On the day Louis was born—January 4, 1809—his father had announced that this child would not become a harness maker but would study books instead.

Even at the age of three, Louis was showing signs that his father's prediction was not unreasonable. He was bright and curious, asking endless questions.

But sitting on the stone floor of the harness shop, young Louis had little thought for the future. He wanted only to play with the scraps of leather that fell to the floor as his father worked. Simon-René had even cut some scraps into shapes for Louis. Tiny leather soldiers, horses, and wagons kept his young son busy while he worked.

Sometimes, however, the shiny tools on the workbench looked more inviting to Louis than the leather toys. Louis longed to copy his father by punching holes in the leather or cutting out the pieces for a harness. But he had been scolded enough times to know that the sharp tools were not meant for young boys to play with.

Then, one day that spring, Simon-René stepped outside the shop to speak with a customer. Louis eyed the sharp tool his father had left on the workbench. Surely there was no harm in poking just one small hole in a piece of material. He grabbed the tool and pushed and poked at the thick leather. His father made the holes easily, but for little Louis, the leather was tough and seemed impossible to get through. He held the piece close to his face and pushed harder.

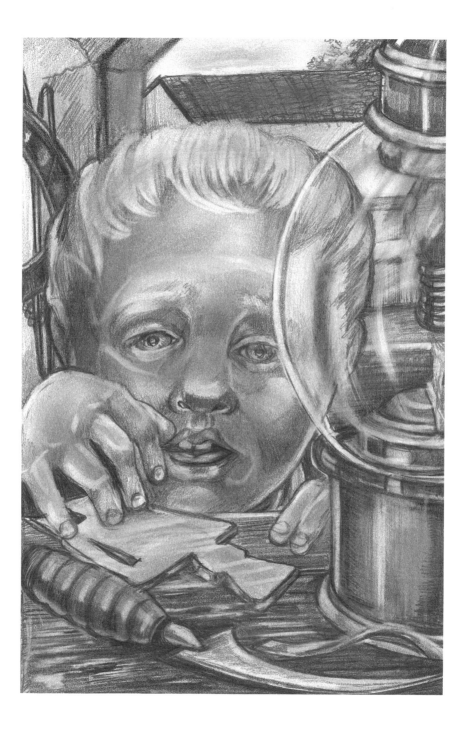

Suddenly the tool slipped from his hand and stabbed him in the left eye.

At the sound of Louis's screams, his father and mother rushed into the shop. Simon-René held a cloth over Louis's bleeding eye while Monique tried to comfort her frightened son.

The Brailles realized immediately that Louis needed medical attention, but there was no hospital in Coupvray, and the closest doctor was miles away. Instead, the Brailles sought the help of a village woman who treated illnesses and injuries with natural medicines made from herbs.

It is not known for sure whether Louis was ever treated by a doctor. In those days, however, even the best doctors knew nothing about killing germs or fighting infections. The village woman's cloth bandage soaked in herbal liquids seemed as good a treatment as any to the worried Brailles.

But the herbal treatments were not enough. Louis's eye grew red and swollen with infection. The love and attention lavished on him by his family couldn't ease his discomfort or keep him from rubbing his injured eye. Within weeks, the infection had spread to Louis's other eye.

The Brailles could only wait and hope for the best. But hope began to fade when Louis continued to ask why the sun wasn't shining outside the kitchen window and why there was no fire in the fireplace. By the fall of 1812, all hope for Louis's recovery was gone. Louis Braille was blind.

2

Finding His Way

Louis sat by the kitchen hearth and listened to his family going about their daily chores. Feet shuffled, doors creaked, and chairs scraped against the stone floor. His sisters offered to take him down to the washhouse. His brother invited him to walk to the village. But for Louis, the once-familiar world outside the farmhouse had become a scary place. The path to the washhouse seemed steep and was covered with roots that might trip him. He was afraid of the cobblestone street, where he could hear but not see the horse-drawn wagons rumbling by.

Simon-René and Monique watched in sorrow as their small son stumbled about the tiny kitchen, bruising his shins on benches and knocking over chairs. They couldn't help but wonder what would become of him. To be blind in France in 1812 meant being helpless, with no way to get an education or earn a living, forever dependent on others. About the best that most blind people could hope for was to make a meager living weaving baskets or playing a musical instrument. Many were forced to become beggars.

But the Brailles were determined that Louis would never have to beg. They would save all the money they could for his future. In the meantime, they knew that Louis had to learn to take care of himself—and that meant stumbling over chairs and bumping into tables for a while.

Simon-René set to work carving a little wooden cane for Louis to use to feel for things that might trip him up. First the boy made his way through the maze of tables and chairs in the farmhouse kitchen, then out into the yard, and gradually up the narrow street to the village. Without his sight, Louis had to rely on his other senses to help him find his way around safely. The clip-clopping of horses and the rumble of wagons warned him to move to the side of the street. The aroma of freshly baked bread led him to the village bakery. The squealing of pigs and hissing of geese told him it was market day. Soon the villagers of Coupvray were used to the sight of Louis Braille tapping his cane along the streets, counting the number of steps it took him to get from the village square to the tailor shop, from the tailor shop to the blacksmith.

By the age of five, Louis had grown accustomed to his dark world. He quickly outgrew his first cane, then his next. His father just kept carving him longer ones. Cane in hand, Louis made his way around so cheerfully and confidently that Monique and Simon-René began to think that maybe there was hope for their son's future after all.

In the winter of 1814, the news reached Coupvray that enemy troops had stopped Napoléon's army at the Rhine River. The French troops retreated toward Paris, and it wasn't long before messengers came to Coupvray with orders for supplies. The villagers were forced to donate hay, oats, bread, cows, and horses for the troops. The Brailles lost their only cow and a supply of vegetables from their garden.

The enemy troops followed Napoléon and defeated him a few months later, and they stayed on in France to keep peace. For the next two years, Coupvray was taken over by the foreign soldiers. The men invaded the villagers' homes, ate their food, and slept in their cellars. Louis hated the heavy tramp of soldiers' boots on the stone floor and the sound of strangers' voices in the farmhouse kitchen.

The troops demanded hot meals from Monique and had no patience with the little blind boy who got in their way. Louis no longer felt safe exploring the village or wandering in the fields and often escaped to the comfort of the harness shop. There, he idled away the days playing with his scrap-leather toys.

In the spring of 1815, when Louis was six years old, a new priest named Jacques Palluy came to Coupvray. Anxious to get acquainted with his new parishioners, Father Palluy spent his first few months visiting each family. Louis was delighted to have a friendly visitor. Although thin and pale, Louis was lively and enthusiastic and kept the young priest entertained with stories and endless questions. Father Palluy came often to the Brailles' home to chat by the fireplace or stroll in the farmyard with Louis.

Realizing how bright his young friend was, the priest asked Louis's parents if he could tutor the boy. They would meet three days a week at the church to study natural science, literature, and religion. The

Brailles were happy for Louis to have a chance to escape the unfriendly soldiers.

Louis memorized the way from his home to the church, tapping his cane and counting his steps along the way. The hours in the church study seemed to fly by as he sat and listened to Father Palluy read poetry, literature, and Bible stories from his leather-bound books. In the sunny courtyard, Louis learned about plants and animals, seasons and stars. The other village children sat in the schoolhouse and learned their science from books. But Louis learned by using his keen senses. Feeling leaves, smelling flowers, and listening closely to birdsongs were all part of his science lessons.

For more than a year, Louis and Father Palluy continued their lessons together. The boy loved the things he was learning from the priest, but he was also curious about the village school. What would it be like to join the other children each morning in the little schoolhouse? When Louis began questioning Father Palluy about the village school, the priest realized that Louis needed more than he was getting from his lessons at the church. He needed to go to school with other children. Louis may have been blind, but he was also bright and eager. He deserved to be taught like the others.

Father Palluy decided to visit Antoine Bécheret, the village schoolmaster. He told Bécheret about his young pupil and asked if the boy could attend school. The schoolmaster was probably surprised at the priest's request. Most blind children in those days received no education at all. To be taught in a school with sighted children was almost unheard of. But Bécheret was a kind and intelligent man who respected Father Palluy. Besides, the Brailles were well known and well liked in the village. Yes, the schoolmaster decided, Louis could attend his school.

Instead of making his way to the church each morning, seven-year-old Louis now waited in the doorway for a classmate to lead him up Touarte Street to the schoolhouse. From his seat in the front row, Louis listened to Bécheret lecture. While the other children took notes, Louis concentrated on memorizing what he heard. When the others worked out math problems on paper, Louis did the figuring in his head.

Louis loved school and did well. But when the time came for reading and writing lessons, Louis was reminded of the difference that set him apart from the other pupils. Why were there no books for him to read? he wondered. Why must he sit alone, bored and frustrated, while the others practiced writing their letters?

At home, Louis's family must have sensed his frustration. There are stories recalling how Simon-René hammered nails into boards in the shape of letters for Louis to trace with his fingers and how Catherine-Joséphine used pieces of straw to spell words on the stone floor for her brother to feel. Louis loved being able to make words and write messages to his family, but he couldn't help envying the other children, who could read stories from real books and write down their lessons.

Louis attended the village school for three years. Although he couldn't read or write, Louis was one of the best students in his class. Father Palluy was pleased to see that his young friend had done so well. He was confident that Louis could accomplish even more if he had the chance.

Bécheret agreed with the priest, but the two men knew that Louis needed a special school—a school designed to help blind people learn. Only one such school existed in France: the Royal Institute for Blind Youth, in Paris. But Louis faced some obstacles. The school was run by the government and attended mainly by children of important families. It was unlikely that the poor son of a harness maker would be accepted. And even if he were, the cost of the school was more than the Brailles could afford.

Determined to see Louis get the education he deserved, Father Palluy asked for help from the Marquis and Marquise d'Orvilliers, wealthy landowners who lived in Coupvray. The marquis and marquise were familiar with the Royal Institute for Blind Youth, and they also knew the boy who tapped his way about the village. They agreed to write to the school on Louis's behalf.

Louis and Father Palluy faced another obstacle as well: convincing Louis's parents. The Brailles listened to the priest describe the school and what it would mean for their son. They knew the value of education and the importance of learning a trade. Still, they couldn't help but worry about sending their ten-year-old son to a city twenty-five miles away. They needed some time to think, they told the priest.

But Louis was impatient. He begged and pleaded with his parents. This school had books, he told them—real books made especially for the blind! Reading straw letters on the kitchen floor was not enough. Only with books would he ever learn about the world. The Brailles knew that Louis was right. They agreed that if he were accepted, they would let him go.

Finally, near the end of January 1819, a letter from the Royal Institute arrived. Not only had Louis been accepted, but he would receive a scholarship! He would attend class and live in the dormitory with the rest of the students, all at no cost to his family. The new school term began in only two weeks. Louis could hardly wait.

3

A New Life

Louis sat beside his father in the carriage as it bounced along the road to Paris. He hoped he looked happy, but inside he was a jumble of butterflies, and his excitement was turning to fear. For the first time in his life, he would be all alone. Could he really get along without the help of his family? To keep from worrying, Louis kept up a lively conversation with his father and had him describe the countryside outside the carriage window.

Simon-René was just as glad for conversation. He, too, had begun to worry. What had he been thinking? Was he crazy to let a ten-year-old boy go away to school in such a big city as Paris? And a blind boy at that! Who would care for Louis the way he and Monique did?

Four hours later, Louis and his father stood in front of a dreary building on rue Saint-Victor (Saint Victor Street). If Louis could have seen the drab, rundown building with its dark, damp hallways and broken windows, he might have turned and fled home to Coupvray. Of course, he could see neither the dreary building nor the shocked and disappointed look on his father's face.

After a brief meeting with Dr. Sebastien Guillié, the school's director, Louis hugged his father good-bye. Then, nervous and afraid, he listened as his father left the school. Now Louis was alone.

For the next few days, Louis struggled to adjust to his new life. He stumbled and groped his way through the maze of narrow halls and winding stairways, running his hands along the cold stone walls in search of his classrooms. The teachers were strict and unfriendly, with rigid rules and harsh punishments. The daily schedule of classes, prayers, and meager meals left little time for anything else but sleep.

At night, lying exhausted on his straw mattress, Louis listened to the unfamiliar noises around him— the whispers of the other boys, the shuffling of feet in the hallway, the rumble of carriages on the cobble- stone street below. Life in Coupvray must have seemed far away. How he must have missed the cozy farmhouse, the fresh country air, the smell of his mother's baking bread, and the pleasant chatter of his family around him. Luckily, just when he needed it most, Louis found a friend—eleven-year-old Gabriel Gauthier.

With Gabriel's help, Louis quickly learned the daily routine of life at the school. Dressed in the school uniform of black wool trousers and a short jacket with brass buttons, Louis ate a breakfast of hot rolls and milk before starting classes in math, gram- mar, history, and Latin.

After hours of sitting quietly, listening to lectures and reciting, Louis looked forward to music lessons in the afternoon. He discovered he had a talent for music and quickly learned to play both the cello and the piano. Unable to read music, the blind students had to memorize the notes. Louis's good memory and ear for music made him one of the best musicians at the institute. Gabriel shared Louis's talent for music, and the two boys grew even closer.

Louis also spent a few hours each week in the school's small workshop. There the students made slippers, purses, and knitted caps, which were sold to earn money to help run the school. Louis liked working with his hands and often daydreamed about the happy times in his father's harness shop.

On Sundays, Louis lined up with the other students for their weekly outing to Mass. Holding a rope in their left hands, they followed their teacher through the crowded streets to a nearby church.

Louis enjoyed his music, did well in his classes, and won an award for his knitting and slipper making. But one thing still bothered him. Where were the special books that Father Palluy had told him about? When was he going to learn to read? Several times he asked to visit the school library, but each time he was told he couldn't.

Maybe Gabriel knew something about it. Sure enough, Gabriel explained to his disappointed friend the simple reason they couldn't visit the library: There was no library. The school had only three books and a few pamphlets that blind people could read.

Only three books? Louis couldn't believe it. There were thousands of books available to the sighted! Three books were better than none, though, Louis figured. He would learn to read those three books. But it wasn't until the start of his second year at the Royal Institute, as a reward for his good grades, that Louis got that chance.

When the day finally came, Louis squirmed with excitement until a servant carried in two big, heavy volumes and placed them on a reading stand in front of the boy.

The books—a volume of French grammar and a prayer book—had been printed using an old printing method called embossing. Heavy, waxed paper was pressed onto pieces of lead shaped into the letters of the alphabet. Each letter became raised on the front side of the page. Two of the heavy pages were then glued together, back to back, so that they could be read like a traditional book. The school's founder, Valentin Haüy, had developed embossed letters that were huge and easy to feel. One sentence could take up a whole page. One paragraph sometimes filled many pages. A complete text would be so long and the pages so thick that the book was usually divided into several volumes.

Louis was disappointed when he realized how different the embossed books were from the small, leather-bound books that had filled the bookshelves in Father Palluy's study. But they were books nonetheless, and Louis was going to read them.

An older student showed Louis how to run his fingers slowly and lightly over the pages, identifying each raised letter as he went along. Louis had a good memory, but it took all his concentration to remember every word. Sometimes by the time he reached the end of a sentence, he forgot the beginning and had to start all over again.

Louis continued to read, but often at night he lay in bed listening to the sounds of the city and thinking about the big, heavy books. After learning how the books were made, he understood why there wasn't a library full of them. They were too bulky to store and too expensive to make. Even worse, they were slow and frustrating to read. Surely there was a better way than embossing to make books for the blind.

Louis began to ask his teachers about other ways the blind might learn to read. Yes, they told him, inventors often came to the school with new ideas. Students had tried some of those ideas in the classroom: wooden letters, strings tied with different knots, and letters carved into wax-coated paper. But none of those methods were practical for making books. So far, Haüy's embossing was the best method of writing and bookmaking available to the blind.

So Louis read and reread the school's three books. But he wanted to read about more than prayers and grammar, and he was ready to do something about it. "If my eyes will not tell me about men and events, ideas and doctrines," Louis wrote in his diary, "I must find another way."

4

Searching for Words

During the summer of 1820, eleven-year-old Louis passed the time making fringes in the harness shop with his father and visiting Father Palluy in town. The fresh country air and Monique's home cooking put some color back into Louis's pale face. He enjoyed the familiar gonging of the big clock in the village square and the aroma of his mother's onion soup. But when the time came to return to school, Louis eagerly boarded the carriage to Paris.

By now, Louis felt at home in the cold, damp school building on rue Saint-Victor. He was used to the stale air, the smell of mildew, the rigorous schedule, and strict rules. But early in 1821, life changed for Louis and the other students. The stern Dr. Guillié was dismissed and replaced by Dr. André Pignier, a kind and understanding man who took an interest in the needs of the students. Dr. Pignier was concerned about the rundown condition of the building and the poor health of many of the students. Right away, he began writing letters to the French government asking that something be done to improve the terrible living conditions. He also relaxed Dr. Guillié's harsh rules and arranged outings to museums and parks to make sure the students got plenty of fresh air.

Shortly after Dr. Pignier's arrival, the halls and dormitories buzzed with excitement. The new director had invited Valentin Haüy, the founder of the school, to visit. There was to be a celebration in honor of the occasion. The students would sing, play music, display their crafts, and demonstrate their reading skills. Louis was one of the students chosen to read. Afterward, he had a chance to meet Haüy. Although the two merely exchanged greetings and shook hands, Louis would never forget meeting the man who had done so much for the blind. He would later describe that meeting as a great inspiration to him.

That same year, an inventor visited the institute with

a method that he thought would help the blind communicate. Charles Barbier, a retired army captain, had invented "night writing," a code used by soldiers to send messages to one another in the dark. Captain Barbier called his invention sonography. A pointed tool was used to punch holes into heavy paper in different combinations of dots and dashes that represented sounds. The combinations were then grouped to form words.

Dr. Pignier was polite but unenthusiastic when he met Barbier. After all, there had been many others before him who had claimed to have developed a way for the blind to read and write. But after seeing a demonstration of Barbier's sonography, Dr. Pignier was more interested. The symbols took up little space and were easy to copy. Maybe there was something to this method! But the director knew that the students would be the best judges of how well this invention worked.

A few days later, Louis and his friend Gabriel sat together in the school auditorium. Like the other students, they talked excitedly about the new invention that was being passed from hand to hand down the rows of seats. They listened to Dr. Pignier describe how sonography worked and had a chance to "read" some messages.

Louis was intrigued. No letters of the alphabet? How could that be? But when he moved his fingers over the raised dots and dashes, he was surprised at how easy it was to feel the combinations. Without having to trace his fingers over each letter, he would be able to read much faster and wouldn't have to struggle so hard to remember what he had already read. Louis left the auditorium that day with one thing on his mind: sonography might be a way to fill the library shelves with books for the blind.

Louis began to spend nearly all of his free time learning sonography. But as he became more familiar with it, he began to find problems. For one thing, a syllable containing several sounds might need nineteen or twenty dots and dashes. A word could have as many as a hundred. That was just too many. Also, the system didn't include numbers or punctuation. The idea was good, but it needed some improvement.

Using a sharp, pointed instrument called a stylus and a slate (a wooden writing board) with heavy paper attached, Louis set out to make some changes to Captain Barbier's invention. "When the day's work was done, and when others were resting," Dr. Pignier later wrote, "I would find [Louis] sitting in some quiet corner with the ruled board, paper, and stylus. Sometimes he would fall asleep in utter weariness."

At the end of the school year, Louis packed his slate and stylus and went home to Coupvray for summer vacation. When Monique and Simon-René greeted their son, they were alarmed by how thin and pale he had become from spending so much time in the damp, drafty school. But they listened with interest when Louis told them about the reading and writing system he was working on.

Louis spent most of the hot summer months of 1822 sitting on the stone steps of the harness shop, combining dots and dashes, reading, revising, and punching some more. By the end of his vacation, Louis had come up with a code that he thought worked better than Barbier's. The main difference between the two was that Louis's combinations of dots and dashes represented letters of the alphabet instead of sounds. That way, Louis thought, the blind could learn to spell and read the same way sighted people did. Because of this change, Louis's code used fewer dots and dashes, making it easier to learn, and his combinations were small enough to fit under a single fingertip, making them quicker to read.

Back at school, Louis rushed straight to Dr. Pignier with his new code. The director was impressed. Maybe his bright young pupil and Captain Barbier could work together to refine the system even more.

But Captain Barbier was outraged when he learned that a thirteen-year-old boy thought his sonography needed changes. His system was good enough to meet the basic needs of the blind. Wasn't that enough?

But Louis was blind himself and knew that it wasn't enough. Blind people wanted more than a system of basic communication. They deserved to have access to literature and science and history. The door to knowledge had been shut for too long.

5

Inventor, Teacher, Musician

One October day in 1824, Louis sat nervously in Dr. Pignier's office. After two years of revising, experimenting, and revising some more, Louis thought he had finally gotten his system right. Besides reducing the number of dots in each grouping, he had decided that dashes were too hard to make and read and had modified the alphabet to use only dots. Then he reduced the number of dots in each cell (a group of dots representing one letter) even more—to six or fewer. He also added punctuation marks, accent marks (important in the French language), numbers, and mathematical symbols. He made sure that every combination of dots could be felt easily with only one finger. Louis was confident that his system was better than Barbier's. He wondered if Dr. Pignier would agree.

Louis sat at Dr. Pignier's desk and punched his stylus into the heavy paper as quickly as the director could read aloud from a newspaper. Then the boy turned the page over and ran his fingers over the raised dots, repeating word for word what Dr. Pignier had just read. The director was amazed. This fifteen-year-old had created a system for reading and writing that was far better than any of the others that had been brought to the school over the years. Louis was relieved at Dr. Pignier's reaction. But next came the most important test of all. Would the other students like it?

When Dr. Pignier presented the dot system to the students, Louis's worries disappeared. The students recognized right away that it was easier to learn and more complete than Barbier's system. An air of excitement filled the dreary corridors of the school as the students talked about Louis's alphabet. Just think of all the new things they could do! They could take notes in class and keep diaries. Best of all, they could do these things by themselves. They wouldn't need a sighted person to help them.

When Dr. Pignier saw the students' response, he decided to try using Louis's system in the classrooms. He had Barbier's sonography equipment changed to accommodate Louis's six-dot cells. The students learned the method quickly.

Now, instead of sitting still in class, struggling to memorize the teachers' lectures, the students hunched over their desks taking notes. "It must be admitted that writing by means of raised dots gave study at the institute a boost," Dr. Pignier wrote. Some of the students even set to work transcribing, or rewriting, parts of the school's embossed books using Louis's system. Transcribing was a very slow process, however, so students still had to use the embossed books as well.

Louis was thrilled that all of his hard work over the last two years was helping his classmates. He was grateful to have the support and encouragement of Dr. Pignier. But he wished he could help the blind outside the school as well. Louis felt strongly that the blind deserved to read and learn on their own and to communicate their ideas to others, just as sighted people did. He was sure that his dot system could help the blind accomplish that.

Dr. Pignier agreed. He wrote to the French government asking that the dot alphabet method be recognized as the official system of writing for the blind. If the government gave its support, Dr. Pignier could probably get money to print new books using the dot alphabet. And maybe if France's only school for the blind was officially using only Louis's system, blind people outside the school would get the chance to learn the system, too.

While Louis waited and hoped for a response, he spent every free minute transcribing parts of the school's embossed books and pamphlets. But no response came. France was still in a state of turmoil after the ousting of Napoléon more than ten years before. Helping the blind was evidently not high on the government's list of important issues.

By 1826, his eighth year at the institute, Louis was busier than ever. In addition to attending classes, he was now acting as a tutor in math, geography, and grammar for some of the younger students. He was also supervising the slipper-making workshop and giving piano lessons.

Louis had begun to play the organ as well. With its double keyboard and rows of stops, the organ was a difficult instrument for a blind musician to play, but Louis became an accomplished performer. Taking turns with other talented organists from the school, Louis played at nearby churches on Sundays.

Louis's days were long and full, but still he continued to experiment with his dot system. Often he punched away with his stylus late into the night. The dormitory was silent except for Louis's hacking cough, which had begun to keep him awake at night.

In October 1828, Louis stood at the head of the class and greeted the new students. Nineteen years old, he was now an assistant teacher, proudly wearing silk and gold braid on his uniform to show his new status. His friend Gabriel and another classmate and friend, Hippolyte Coltat, had also been appointed assistant teachers. Because they were blind, the three friends understood their students better than teachers who could see.

Louis's classes, in particular, were popular with the students. Hippolyte later wrote that Louis taught with "charm and wisdom." "Monsieur Braille" was especially kind to the newest students. Nine years had passed since he had first arrived at the institute. But Louis had never forgotten the feeling of being new there, groping his way along the unfamiliar hallways, and he did all he could to make the students feel at home.

Sometimes Louis took a break from his work to go for walks with Gabriel and Hippolyte. He especially enjoyed the botanical gardens. But not even the exercise or fresh air seemed to relieve the fatigue and persistent cough that continued to plague him.

It had been four years since Louis first showed his dot system to Dr. Pignier, but still the director's efforts to gain official recognition of the system had gotten no results. Many government officials believed that blind people should use the same alphabet as the sighted. Besides, transcribing books into a new system would be expensive.

All Louis could do was continue transcribing reading material and making small improvements to his system. Most important of those improvements was adding symbols for musical notation. For the first time, blind musicians had a way to read music and write it down.

In 1829, when Louis was twenty years old, he published a short book with a long title: *Method of Writing Words, Music and Plain Songs by Means of Dots, for Use by the Blind and Arranged for Them.* The book gave a detailed description of the six-dot system and was printed using the embossed method so it could be read by both the blind and the sighted.

In May 1831, Louis received the bad news that his father had died. Louis spent a few days in Coupvray attending the funeral and helping his brother see to the family's affairs. Even though Louis supported himself with his teaching job, Simon-René had still worried about his blind son's future. In his will, he left the family farmhouse and money earned by the vineyards to Louis, although Monique would continue to live there and oversee the farm. In addition, shortly before his death, Simon-René had sent a letter to Dr. Pignier asking him to continue to look after Louis and to allow him to stay on at the institute. Dr. Pignier had assured the Brailles that Louis's future with the school was secure.

Two years later, Louis, Gabriel, and Hippolyte were promoted to full-fledged teachers at the school. That same year, Louis was offered a position as organist at St. Nicholas-des-Champs, one of the largest churches in Paris. Louis gladly accepted the position. Playing the church organ was a chance for him to combine his religious faith with his love of music. Although his schedule would now be even busier, Louis thought he could handle it.

6

Opening the Door

Louis arrived at the 1834 Exhibition of Industry nervous but hopeful. Held in a large open square in the heart of Paris, the exhibition was to feature inventions and discoveries of all kinds. Dr. Pignier had arranged for Louis to demonstrate his dot system there. Thousands of people, including the king of France, Louis Philippe, were expected to visit the exhibits. That was reason enough to be nervous! But Louis was also hopeful that after seeing his system demonstrated, the king would finally give it official recognition.

All day, Louis used his stylus to write down whatever spectators told him to. Then, as his hand darted across the paper, he read back the dictation as quickly as any sighted person could read. King Louis Philippe witnessed one of the demonstrations. With him was the minister of the interior—the very man to whom Dr. Pignier had written on Louis's behalf. Louis was anxious to hear their reaction. The men praised him and complimented him on his fine work—but that was all.

Louis was devastated. Praise and compliments were fine, but they would not make his dot system the official written language for the blind. The students at the institute would continue to learn Haüy's slow and inadequate embossed alphabet. Without government funds to help pay for books to be printed in the dot alphabet, the library would grow only if Louis and the students transcribed the books themselves. And without government support, the dot system would remain within the school. Other blind people throughout France and the rest of the world would remain cut off from a source of useful, independent communication. Louis left the exhibition feeling hopeless about the future of his method.

Back at school, Louis's busy schedule helped raise his spirits. But he had another worry that nothing could cover up. Over the last few years, he had become more frail, and the bouts of fatigue, coughing, and fever he had been suffering were getting worse. A brief vacation in Coupvray usually helped his cough, but once he returned to the school, his cough would come back.

By 1835, Louis realized that his condition was serious. After one particularly bad night of fever and coughing, he called in the school doctor. The diagnosis wasn't good. Twenty-six-year-old Louis was suffering from consumption, a serious illness now known as tuberculosis, or TB. In those days, there was no cure for TB. The only treatment was fresh air and rest.

Louis tried both. He cut back on his teaching schedule and spent more time outside. While he rested, he continued to tinker with his dot alphabet. In 1836, he added the letter *W* so his six-dot code could be used to write in English. (*W* isn't used in the French language.) He also worked on ways to produce math textbooks for blind students. He would later publish a book of his ideas called *A Little Synopsis of Arithmetic for Beginners.*

In 1837, the first full-length book written in the dot alphabet system was completed and added to the school library. Titled *A Summary of French History, Century by Century* (thought to have been written by Father Philippe Anaclet), the book consisted of three volumes, each of which held over two hundred pages. Students and teachers at the school had made the book by hand in their free time. It had taken them nearly two years. Louis must have been proud and honored. One book didn't add up to the shelves of volumes he had imagined as a child, but it was a start.

Louis had made many improvements to his dot system over the years, but he still hoped he could develop a way for the blind and the sighted to communicate in writing. It seemed impractical to expect that sighted people would learn the dot system, yet there was no way around the fact that the blind couldn't read standard printed type. By 1839, Louis had come up with a solution to the problem. He developed an entirely new system of writing called raphigraphy, which used raised dots to form the shapes of alphabet letters. Louis's system could be easily read by the sighted, and it was still more compact and easier to make and read than Haüy's embossed letters.

Two years later, a blind friend of Louis's, François-Pierre Foucault, invented a method of printing raphigraphy. Operated somewhat like a typewriter, the printing press had metal keys that, when pressed, left raised dots in the paper. Now writing to the sighted was quick and simple. Louis had his own raphigraphy machine in his room for writing home to his mother. He later adapted the machine for composing music.

In the spring of 1840, Louis was faced with a terrible disappointment. Dr. Pignier was fired from his position as director of the school. To take his place, the French government chose P. Armand Dufau, Dr. Pignier's assistant and a former teacher at the school. Dufau had convinced the government that Pignier's liberal political views were having a bad influence on the students. Almost immediately, life at the school changed. As in earlier times under Dr. Guillié, rules were harsh and punishments severe.

A few weeks later, Louis suffered another devastating blow. Dufau announced that Louis's method would no longer be permitted in the institute's classrooms. Dufau believed that a special alphabet would set the blind apart from the sighted even more. But another reason lay behind Dufau's decision. He worried that the alphabet would give the blind students and teachers too much independence and threaten the jobs of the school's sighted teachers.

The place Louis had called home for most of his life was now a source of sadness. His spirits sank, and his health worsened. Early in 1843, evidence of bleeding in his lungs forced him to return to Coupvray to rest. Once again, the fresh country air and the care of his mother revived his spirits as well as his strength.

Life on the farm was a welcome change from the

dreary atmosphere at school. Louis wrote to his friend Gabriel, "If you ever come to visit me in Coupvray, I shall teach you how to milk a cow!"

That summer, Louis sat in the doorway of the harness shop (now run by his nephews) and transcribed books and music. He would not let Dufau's disapproval of his work stop him.

In the fall, when Louis returned to Paris, the worried voices of his friends told him something was wrong. Reluctantly, they gave him the bad news. Dufau had been studying methods for teaching the blind in other parts of Europe and had decided to change the size and shape of Haüy's embossed alphabet. While Louis was away, Dufau had burned all of the school's embossed books. Louis was horrified. Although embossed books weren't ideal, the lack of materials available to blind people had made them priceless. Now Dufau had reduced them to ashes in the school courtyard.

Dufau also banned all use of the dot alphabet outside the classrooms as well as inside. He thought this would force the students to accept his ideas. He was wrong. The students continued using Louis's method whenever they could. Late at night, papers rustled and students whispered as they punched notes, journals, and letters. They even taught the method to the newer and younger students. When a student was caught, punishment was severe—no dinner, a whack with a ruler, or even time spent locked up alone.

Louis must have been discouraged. Luckily, he had a supporter willing to help. Joseph Guadet, Dufau's assistant, had come to the institute in 1840. He had seen that the students preferred the dot alphabet and had even learned to read and write it himself (the first sighted person to do so).

Guadet was determined to convince Dufau to reconsider his ban of the dot alphabet. The students' loyalty to the method should not be ignored, he told Dufau. After all, weren't they the best judges of how well the alphabet system worked? Shouldn't they be the ones to decide how they wanted to read and write? Besides, the system was easy to learn and transcribe, and cheaper to print than embossing. Guadet didn't know if his arguments were persuading the stubborn director, but at least Dufau was listening.

Louis was becoming frailer all the time, suffering fits of coughing that left him exhausted. The years spent in the school had made his condition worse and had most likely contributed to the poor health of many of the other teachers and students as well. (Louis's longtime friend Gabriel also suffered from tuberculosis.) Although Dr. Pignier had fought hard to improve the living conditions of the students, it wasn't until November 1843, several years after he had left, that the Royal Institute got a new home: a clean, airy building on the boulevard des Invalides.

At the dedication of the new building on February 22, 1844, the auditorium was filled with family members, friends, government officials, and French citizens who had donated money for the new school. Louis sat with the other teachers and the students and listened to speeches, music, and poetry. Then Guadet walked to the podium and read from a booklet that he had written himself. It was titled *An Account of the System of Raised Dots for Use by the Blind.* Imagine Louis's surprise! Guadet had finally convinced Dufau to lift the ban on the dot method! Louis sat in stunned silence as Guadet finished his reading and began to demonstrate the dot alphabet to the audience. Afterward, Guadet introduced Louis as the method's creator. The students were thrilled, too. Now if only Louis could get his alphabet beyond the walls of the school.

But Louis didn't have much strength left for such struggles. By 1850, his health forced him to give up teaching except for a few music lessons. Although he spent most of his time in bed, Louis kept busy transcribing books. The little library was slowly growing.

In December 1851, Louis was so weak and his lungs so bad that he was confined to the school infirmary. His old friends Gabriel, Hippolyte, and Dr. Pignier visited him often. Louis knew he was dying and calmly told his friends, "I am convinced that my mission is finished on earth." Louis died on January 6, 1852, two days after his forty-third birthday.

Two years after Louis's death, in 1854, the French government finally approved the dot system, which was to become known simply as "braille." In 1878, representatives of most of the European countries met at the World Congress for the Blind. Together they voted to make braille the standard system of reading and writing for the blind throughout the world.

Still, it took a while for the braille system to catch on outside of Europe. In the United States, braille was first introduced in 1860 at the Missouri School for the Blind. However, other dot alphabets were also used in the United States until 1917, when braille was adopted as the official system. In 1949, the United Nations Education, Scientific, and Cultural Organization (UNESCO) adopted a standard braille code that had potential for use in all languages. Since then, braille has been adapted for use in almost every major language in the world. Nearly everything published for the sighted is available in braille, from novels to cookbooks to phone books. Braille has made it possible for blind people to play cards and board games, read music, type on computer keyboards, and read printouts of their work.

Louis Braille's contribution to the world is perhaps best summarized in the words on the plaque in Coupvray's village square (now known as Louis Braille Square): "He opened the door to knowledge for all those who cannot see."

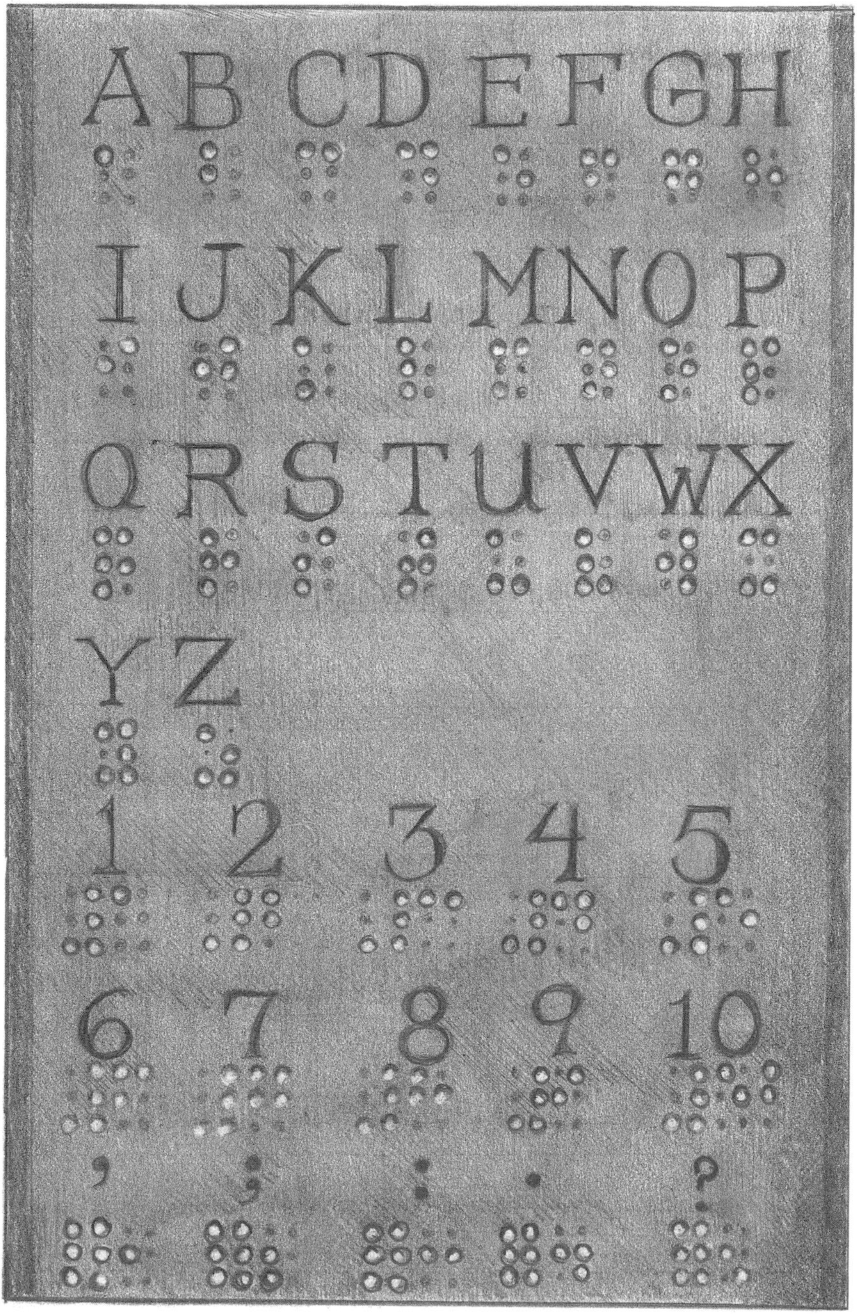
A B C D E F G H
I J K L M N O P
Q R S T U V W X
Y Z
1 2 3 4 5
6 7 8 9 10
, ; : . ?

Bibliography

Bickel, Lennard. *Triumph over Darkness: The Life of Louis Braille.* Anstey, England: F. A. Thorpe Ltd., 1988.

Birch, Beverley. *Louis Braille.* Milwaukee: Gareth Stevens, 1989.

Bryant, Jennifer Fisher. *Louis Braille: Teacher of the Blind.* New York: Chelsea House, 1994.

Degering, Etta. *Seeing Fingers: The Story of Louis Braille.* New York: David McKay Company, 1962.

Keeler, Stephen. *Louis Braille.* New York: Bookwright, 1986.

Neimark, Anne E. *Touch of Light: The Story of Louis Braille.* New York: Harcourt, Brace, and World, Inc., 1970.

Roblin, Jean. *The Reading Fingers: Life of Louis Braille.* Translated by Ruth G. Mandalian. New York: American Foundation for the Blind, 1955.

Wise, Janet. *Dot Writing: A Manual of English Braille.* New York: Janet Wise Publisher, 1960.

Index

About the Author

In addition to the life of famous Frenchman Louis Braille, **Barbara O'Connor** has researched and recorded the lives of an Italian teacher, a worldly modern dancer, and a beloved American journalist. *Mammolina: A Story about Maria Montessori; Barefoot Dancer: The Story of Isadora Duncan;* and *The Soldiers' Voice: The Story of Ernie Pyle* are all published by Carolrhoda Books.

When she is not writing, Ms. O'Connor enjoys gardening, tap dancing, walking with her trusty dog, Murphy, and playing Nintendo. She lives with her husband, Bill, and son, Grady, in Duxbury, Massachusetts.

About the Illustrator

Rochelle Draper is a freelance writer, illustrator, and art teacher. This is the third biography she has illustrated for Carolrhoda Books. Her first two books, *Georgia O'Keeffe* and *Vincent van Gogh,* are part of the On My Own series for beginning readers. In her free time, Ms. Draper enjoys cooking, reading, entertaining, and spending quiet time with her husband and three children. She lives with her family on a hobby farm in central Minnesota.